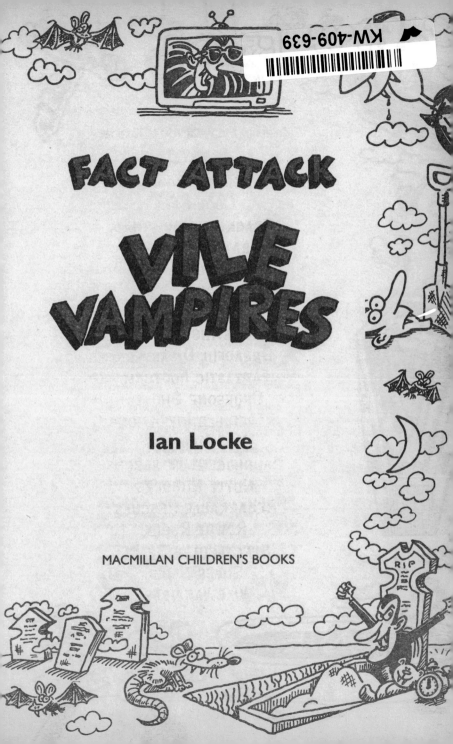

FACT ATTACK

VILE VAMPIRES

Ian Locke

MACMILLAN CHILDREN'S BOOKS

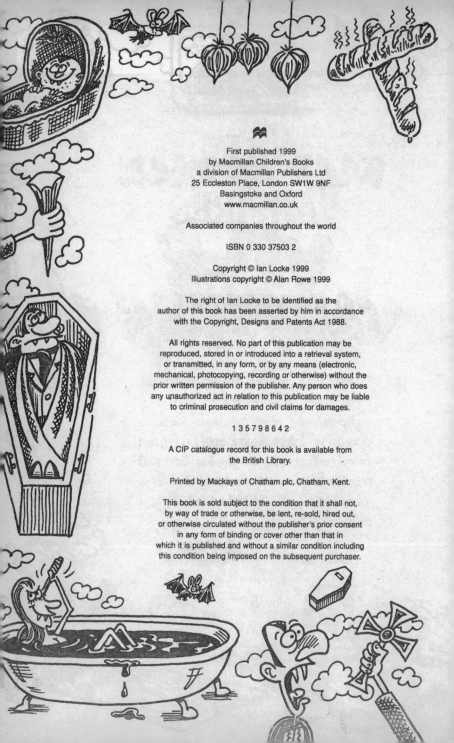

First published 1999
by Macmillan Children's Books
a division of Macmillan Publishers Ltd
25 Eccleston Place, London SW1W 9NF
Basingstoke and Oxford
www.macmillan.co.uk

Associated companies throughout the world

ISBN 0 330 37503 2

1 3 5 7 9 8 6 4 2

A CIP catalogue record for this book is available from
the British Library.

Printed by Mackays of Chatham plc, Chatham, Kent.

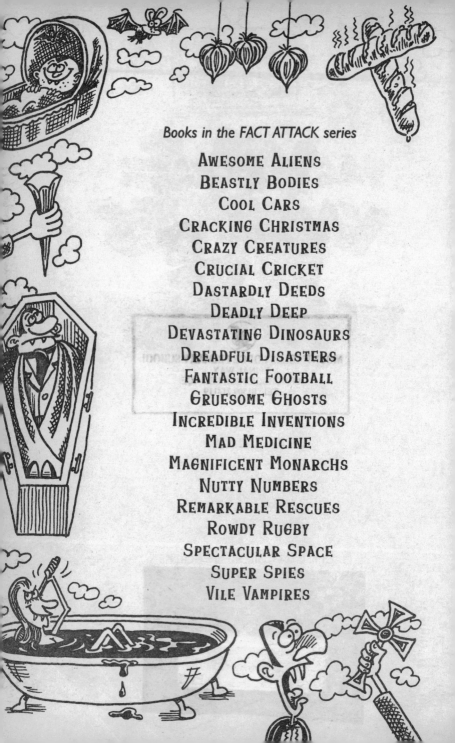

Books in the FACT ATTACK series

VILE VAMPIRES

DID YOU KNOW THAT . . .

★ In the first stories about vampires, told over 2,000 years ago, the vampire was said to have been a dragon who ate the moon. The legend came to Europe from the Far East and stories began to be told of vampires who sucked the blood of babies and people.

5

★ There are different sorts of vampires, according to stories from Romania, Russia, Bulgaria, Moravia, China and Mexico.

★ From very early on, vampires, ghosts, werewolves and spirits were known as the 'undead'. Only in the 1400s were the different types of the 'undead' defined.

★ There are nine ghostly kings, queens and princes in Britain:
1. Queen Isabella.
2. Anne Boleyn.
3. King Edward I.
4. Queen Catherine Howard.
5. Elizabeth I.
6. Queen Catherine of Aragon.
7. Mary, Queen of Scots.
8. Queen Maude (or Mab).
9. Bonnie Prince Charlie.

6

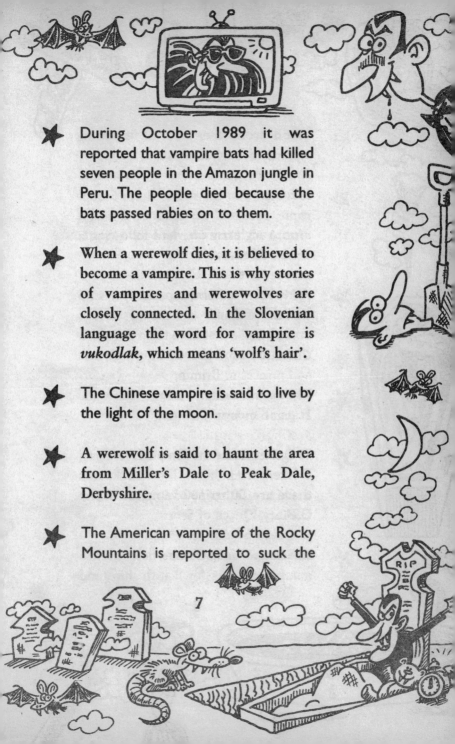

★ During October 1989 it was reported that vampire bats had killed seven people in the Amazon jungle in Peru. The people died because the bats passed rabies on to them.

★ When a werewolf dies, it is believed to become a vampire. This is why stories of vampires and werewolves are closely connected. In the Slovenian language the word for vampire is *vukodlak*, which means 'wolf's hair'.

★ The Chinese vampire is said to live by the light of the moon.

★ A werewolf is said to haunt the area from Miller's Dale to Peak Dale, Derbyshire.

★ The American vampire of the Rocky Mountains is reported to suck the

blood from the ears of its living victims through its nose!

★ It is said that the writer Bram Stoker came up with the idea of *Dracula* after a nightmare he had following a dinner of crabs.

★ A Mexican vampire apparently has no skin on its skull – like the mysterious crystal skulls that have been dug up in the past.

★ The word vampire comes from the Hungarian word, *vampir*.

★ The director of the Vampire Research Center, in Elmhurst, New York, says there are 80 to 100 vampires in the USA.

★ The name Vampire has been used a number of times for British ships and

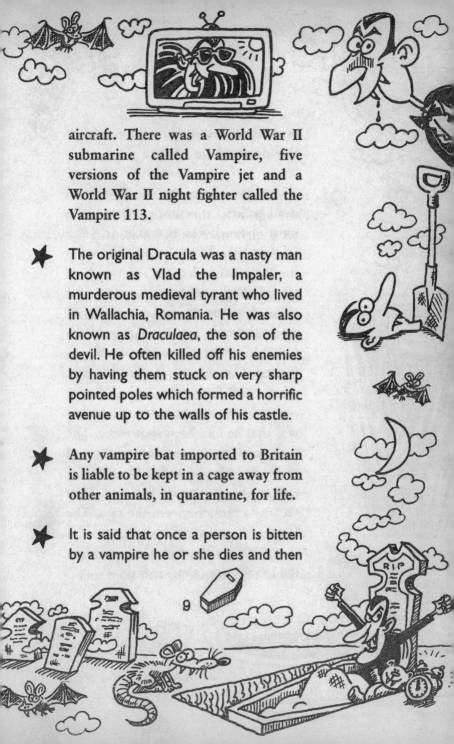

aircraft. There was a World War II submarine called Vampire, five versions of the Vampire jet and a World War II night fighter called the Vampire 113.

★ The original Dracula was a nasty man known as Vlad the Impaler, a murderous medieval tyrant who lived in Wallachia, Romania. He was also known as *Draculaea*, the son of the devil. He often killed off his enemies by having them stuck on very sharp pointed poles which formed a horrific avenue up to the walls of his castle.

★ Any vampire bat imported to Britain is liable to be kept in a cage away from other animals, in quarantine, for life.

★ It is said that once a person is bitten by a vampire he or she dies and then

9

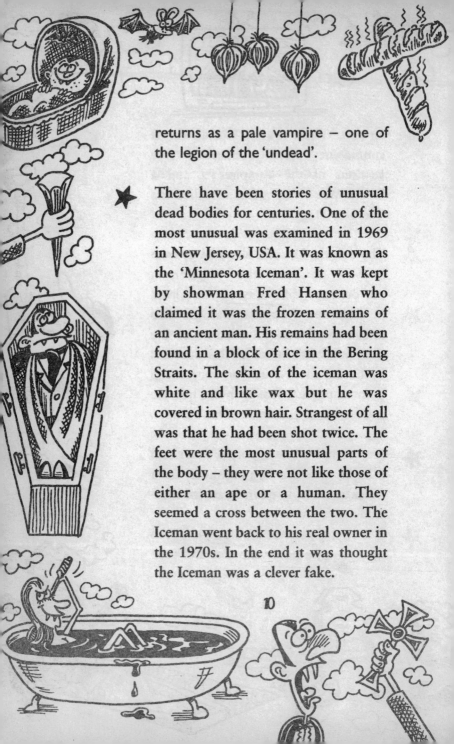

returns as a pale vampire – one of the legion of the 'undead'.

★ There have been stories of unusual dead bodies for centuries. One of the most unusual was examined in 1969 in New Jersey, USA. It was known as the 'Minnesota Iceman'. It was kept by showman Fred Hansen who claimed it was the frozen remains of an ancient man. His remains had been found in a block of ice in the Bering Straits. The skin of the iceman was white and like wax but he was covered in brown hair. Strangest of all was that he had been shot twice. The feet were the most unusual parts of the body – they were not like those of either an ape or a human. They seemed a cross between the two. The Iceman went back to his real owner in the 1970s. In the end it was thought the Iceman was a clever fake.

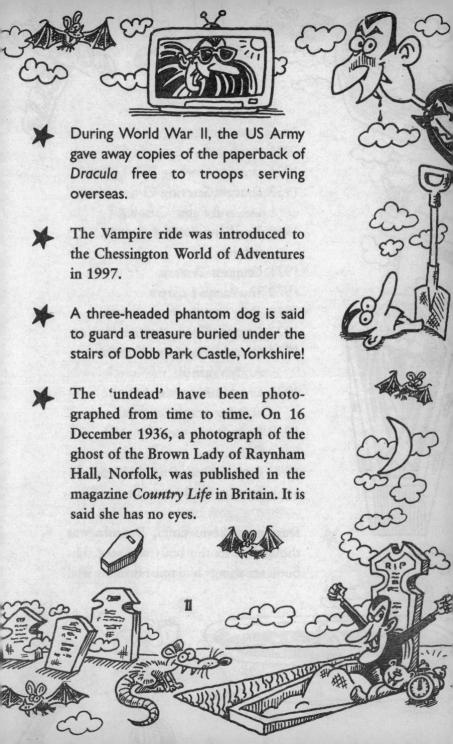

★ During World War II, the US Army gave away copies of the paperback of *Dracula* free to troops serving overseas.

★ The Vampire ride was introduced to the Chessington World of Adventures in 1997.

★ A three-headed phantom dog is said to guard a treasure buried under the stairs of Dobb Park Castle, Yorkshire!

★ The 'undead' have been photographed from time to time. On 16 December 1936, a photograph of the ghost of the Brown Lady of Raynham Hall, Norfolk, was published in the magazine *Country Life* in Britain. It is said she has no eyes.

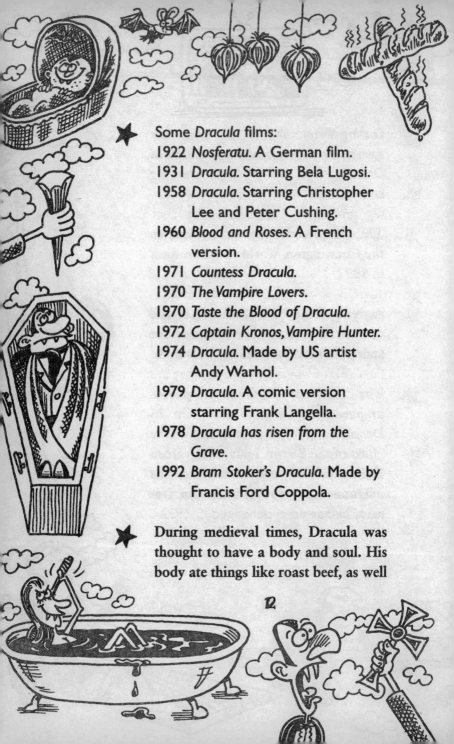

★ Some *Dracula* films:

1922 *Nosferatu*. A German film.

1931 *Dracula*. Starring Bela Lugosi.

1958 *Dracula*. Starring Christopher Lee and Peter Cushing.

1960 *Blood and Roses*. A French version.

1971 *Countess Dracula*.

1970 *The Vampire Lovers*.

1970 *Taste the Blood of Dracula*.

1972 *Captain Kronos, Vampire Hunter*.

1974 *Dracula*. Made by US artist Andy Warhol.

1979 *Dracula*. A comic version starring Frank Langella.

1978 *Dracula has risen from the Grave*.

1992 *Bram Stoker's Dracula*. Made by Francis Ford Coppola.

★ During medieval times, Dracula was thought to have a body and soul. His body ate things like roast beef, as well

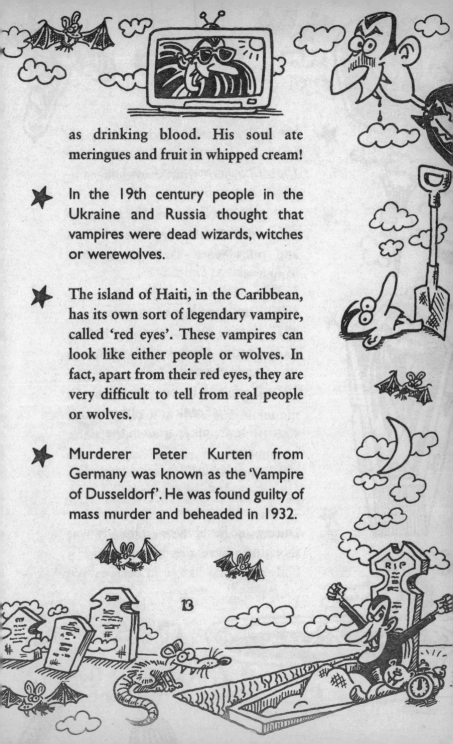

as drinking blood. His soul ate meringues and fruit in whipped cream!

★ In the 19th century people in the Ukraine and Russia thought that vampires were dead wizards, witches or werewolves.

★ The island of Haiti, in the Caribbean, has its own sort of legendary vampire, called 'red eyes'. These vampires can look like either people or wolves. In fact, apart from their red eyes, they are very difficult to tell from real people or wolves.

★ Murderer Peter Kurten from Germany was known as the 'Vampire of Dusseldorf'. He was found guilty of mass murder and beheaded in 1932.

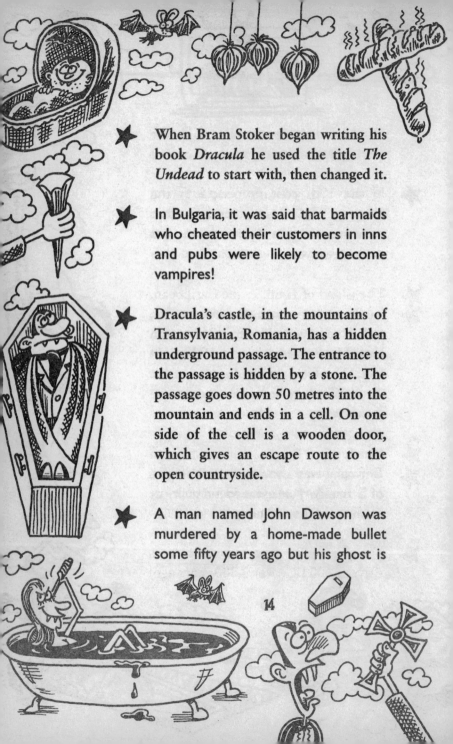

When Bram Stoker began writing his book *Dracula* he used the title *The Undead* to start with, then changed it.

In Bulgaria, it was said that barmaids who cheated their customers in inns and pubs were likely to become vampires!

Dracula's castle, in the mountains of Transylvania, Romania, has a hidden underground passage. The entrance to the passage is hidden by a stone. The passage goes down 50 metres into the mountain and ends in a cell. On one side of the cell is a wooden door, which gives an escape route to the open countryside.

A man named John Dawson was murdered by a home-made bullet some fifty years ago but his ghost is

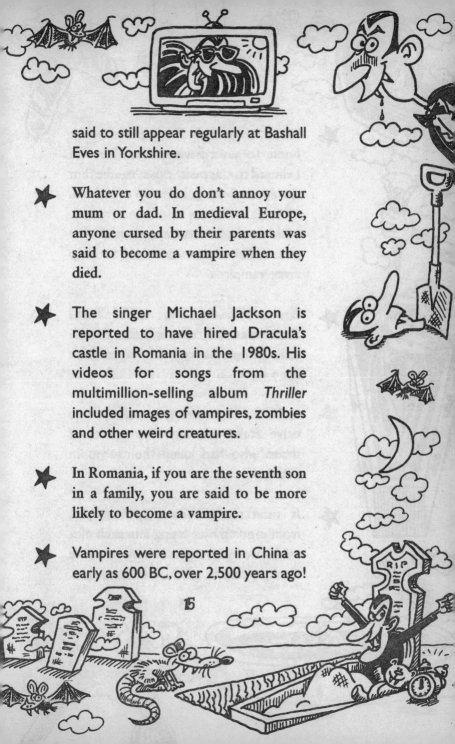

said to still appear regularly at Bashall Eves in Yorkshire.

Whatever you do don't annoy your mum or dad. In medieval Europe, anyone cursed by their parents was said to become a vampire when they died.

The singer Michael Jackson is reported to have hired Dracula's castle in Romania in the 1980s. His videos for songs from the multimillion-selling album *Thriller* included images of vampires, zombies and other weird creatures.

In Romania, if you are the seventh son in a family, you are said to be more likely to become a vampire.

Vampires were reported in China as early as 600 BC, over 2,500 years ago!

15

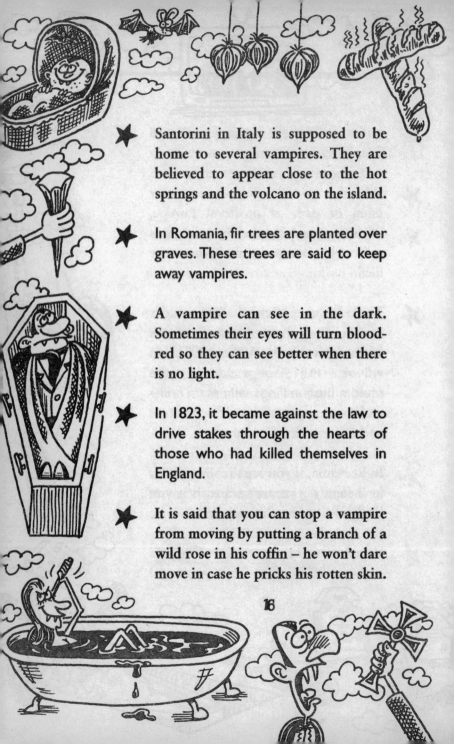

★ Santorini in Italy is supposed to be home to several vampires. They are believed to appear close to the hot springs and the volcano on the island.

★ In Romania, fir trees are planted over graves. These trees are said to keep away vampires.

★ A vampire can see in the dark. Sometimes their eyes will turn blood-red so they can see better when there is no light.

★ In 1823, it became against the law to drive stakes through the hearts of those who had killed themselves in England.

★ It is said that you can stop a vampire from moving by putting a branch of a wild rose in his coffin – he won't dare move in case he pricks his rotten skin.

16

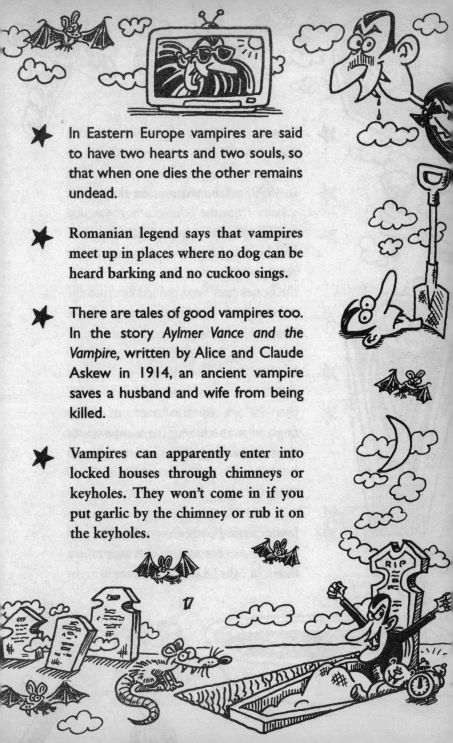

★ In Eastern Europe vampires are said to have two hearts and two souls, so that when one dies the other remains undead.

★ Romanian legend says that vampires meet up in places where no dog can be heard barking and no cuckoo sings.

★ There are tales of good vampires too. In the story *Aylmer Vance and the Vampire*, written by Alice and Claude Askew in 1914, an ancient vampire saves a husband and wife from being killed.

★ Vampires can apparently enter into locked houses through chimneys or keyholes. They won't come in if you put garlic by the chimney or rub it on the keyholes.

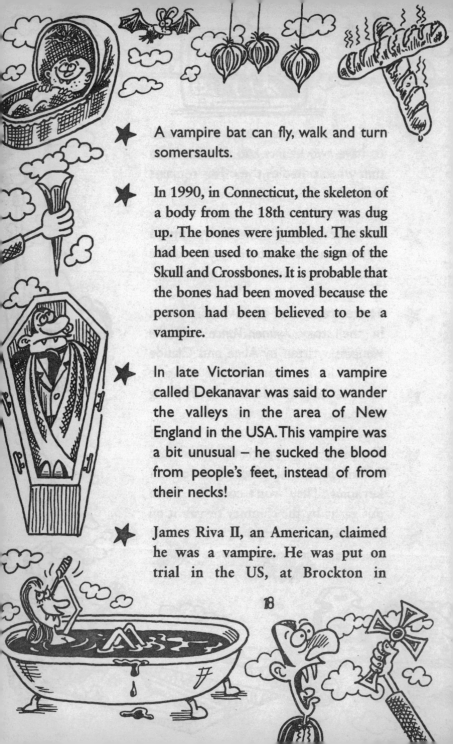

A vampire bat can fly, walk and turn somersaults.

In 1990, in Connecticut, the skeleton of a body from the 18th century was dug up. The bones were jumbled. The skull had been used to make the sign of the Skull and Crossbones. It is probable that the bones had been moved because the person had been believed to be a vampire.

In late Victorian times a vampire called Dekanavar was said to wander the valleys in the area of New England in the USA. This vampire was a bit unusual – he sucked the blood from people's feet, instead of from their necks!

James Riva II, an American, claimed he was a vampire. He was put on trial in the US, at Brockton in

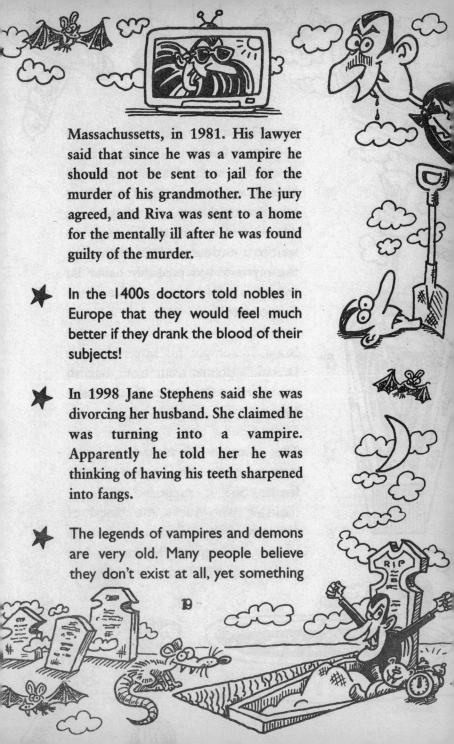

Massachussetts, in 1981. His lawyer said that since he was a vampire he should not be sent to jail for the murder of his grandmother. The jury agreed, and Riva was sent to a home for the mentally ill after he was found guilty of the murder.

★ In the 1400s doctors told nobles in Europe that they would feel much better if they drank the blood of their subjects!

★ In 1998 Jane Stephens said she was divorcing her husband. She claimed he was turning into a vampire. Apparently he told her he was thinking of having his teeth sharpened into fangs.

★ The legends of vampires and demons are very old. Many people believe they don't exist at all, yet something

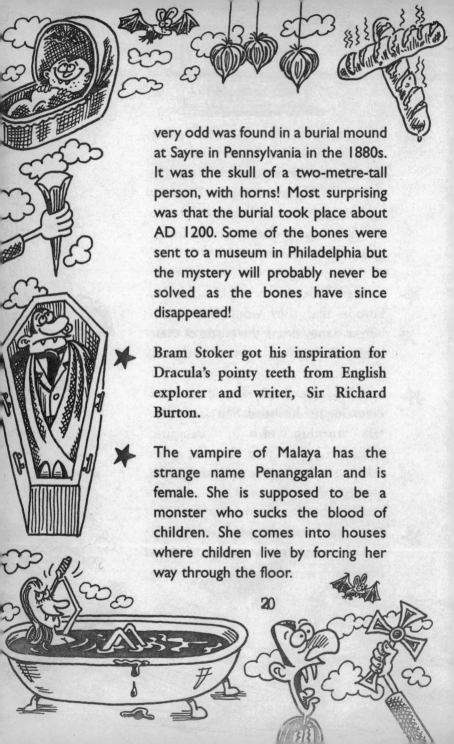

very odd was found in a burial mound at Sayre in Pennsylvania in the 1880s. It was the skull of a two-metre-tall person, with horns! Most surprising was that the burial took place about AD 1200. Some of the bones were sent to a museum in Philadelphia but the mystery will probably never be solved as the bones have since disappeared!

★ Bram Stoker got his inspiration for Dracula's pointy teeth from English explorer and writer, Sir Richard Burton.

★ The vampire of Malaya has the strange name Penanggalan and is female. She is supposed to be a monster who sucks the blood of children. She comes into houses where children live by forcing her way through the floor.

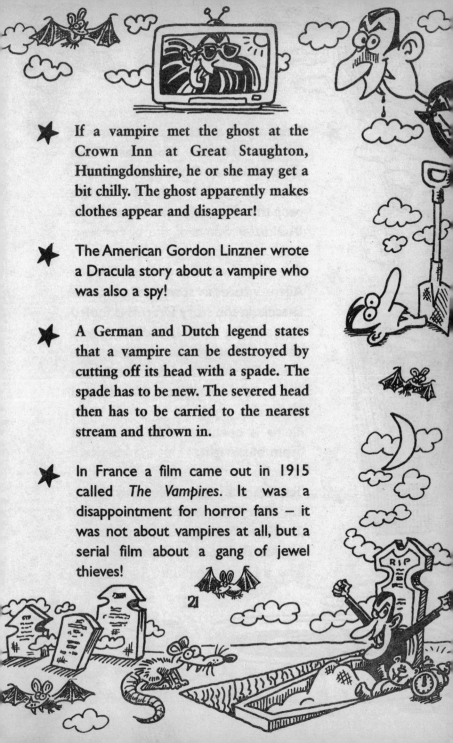

★ If a vampire met the ghost at the Crown Inn at Great Staughton, Huntingdonshire, he or she may get a bit chilly. The ghost apparently makes clothes appear and disappear!

★ The American Gordon Linzner wrote a Dracula story about a vampire who was also a spy!

★ A German and Dutch legend states that a vampire can be destroyed by cutting off its head with a spade. The spade has to be new. The severed head then has to be carried to the nearest stream and thrown in.

★ In France a film came out in 1915 called *The Vampires*. It was a disappointment for horror fans – it was not about vampires at all, but a serial film about a gang of jewel thieves!

21

Bela Lugosi, the Hungarian actor who became famous for his film appearances as Dracula in the USA, never learned to speak English properly. His real name was Bela Blasko.

The American film director Woody Allen wrote a story called *Count Dracula*. In the story Dracula is fooled into arriving early at a dinner party because of an eclipse of the sun. He tries very hard to leave the house and avoid the daylight but he is killed when the cupboard in which he is hiding is opened and he is hit by a beam of sunlight.

Ten Dracula books with funny titles:
1. *What Time is it, Dracula?*
2. *Friendly Fangs*
3. *My Friend, the Vampire*

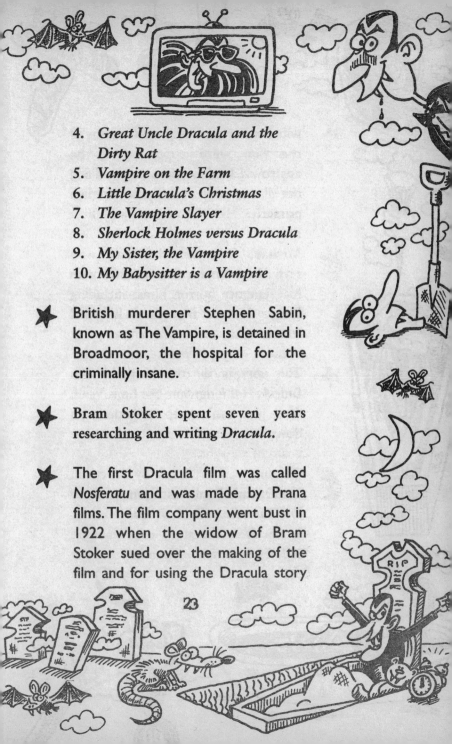

4. *Great Uncle Dracula and the Dirty Rat*
5. *Vampire on the Farm*
6. *Little Dracula's Christmas*
7. *The Vampire Slayer*
8. *Sherlock Holmes versus Dracula*
9. *My Sister, the Vampire*
10. *My Babysitter is a Vampire*

★ British murderer Stephen Sabin, known as The Vampire, is detained in Broadmoor, the hospital for the criminally insane.

★ Bram Stoker spent seven years researching and writing *Dracula*.

★ The first Dracula film was called *Nosferatu* and was made by Prana films. The film company went bust in 1922 when the widow of Bram Stoker sued over the making of the film and for using the Dracula story

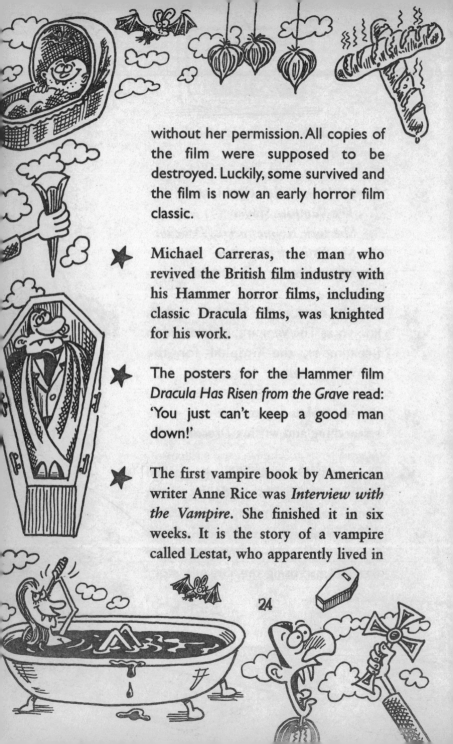

without her permission. All copies of the film were supposed to be destroyed. Luckily, some survived and the film is now an early horror film classic.

★ Michael Carreras, the man who revived the British film industry with his Hammer horror films, including classic Dracula films, was knighted for his work.

★ The posters for the Hammer film *Dracula Has Risen from the Grave* read: 'You just can't keep a good man down!'

★ The first vampire book by American writer Anne Rice was *Interview with the Vampire*. She finished it in six weeks. It is the story of a vampire called Lestat, who apparently lived in

24

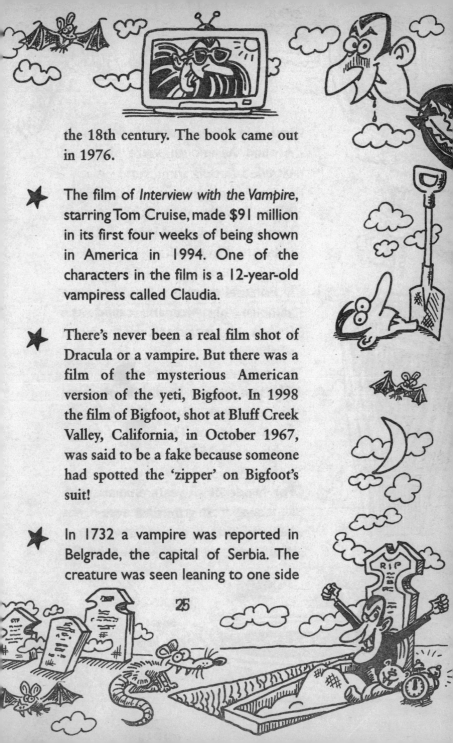

the 18th century. The book came out in 1976.

⭐ The film of *Interview with the Vampire*, starring Tom Cruise, made $91 million in its first four weeks of being shown in America in 1994. One of the characters in the film is a 12-year-old vampiress called Claudia.

⭐ There's never been a real film shot of Dracula or a vampire. But there was a film of the mysterious American version of the yeti, Bigfoot. In 1998 the film of Bigfoot, shot at Bluff Creek Valley, California, in October 1967, was said to be a fake because someone had spotted the 'zipper' on Bigfoot's suit!

⭐ In 1732 a vampire was reported in Belgrade, the capital of Serbia. The creature was seen leaning to one side

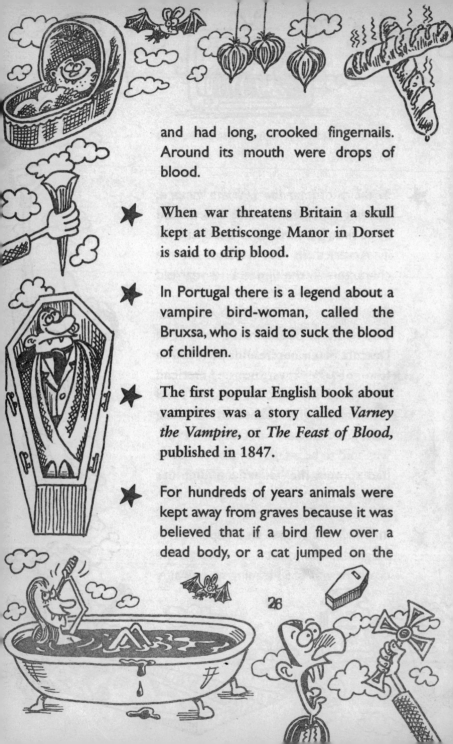

and had long, crooked fingernails. Around its mouth were drops of blood.

★ When war threatens Britain a skull kept at Bettisconge Manor in Dorset is said to drip blood.

★ In Portugal there is a legend about a vampire bird-woman, called the Bruxsa, who is said to suck the blood of children.

★ The first popular English book about vampires was a story called *Varney the Vampire*, or *The Feast of Blood*, published in 1847.

★ For hundreds of years animals were kept away from graves because it was believed that if a bird flew over a dead body, or a cat jumped on the

26

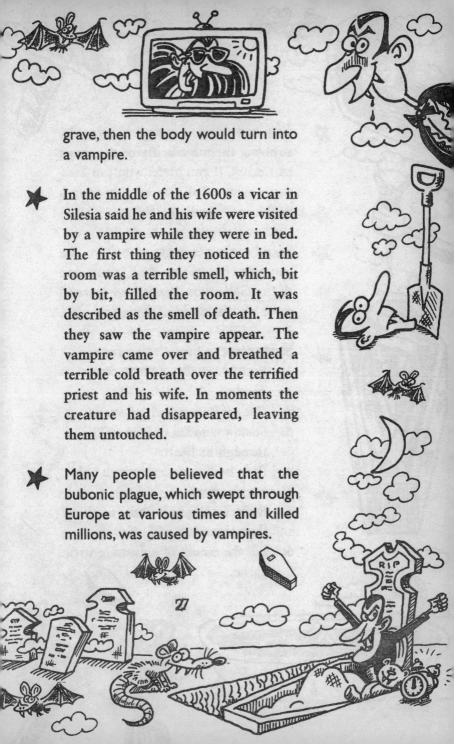

grave, then the body would turn into a vampire.

★ In the middle of the 1600s a vicar in Silesia said he and his wife were visited by a vampire while they were in bed. The first thing they noticed in the room was a terrible smell, which, bit by bit, filled the room. It was described as the smell of death. Then they saw the vampire appear. The vampire came over and breathed a terrible cold breath over the terrified priest and his wife. In moments the creature had disappeared, leaving them untouched.

★ Many people believed that the bubonic plague, which swept through Europe at various times and killed millions, was caused by vampires.

27

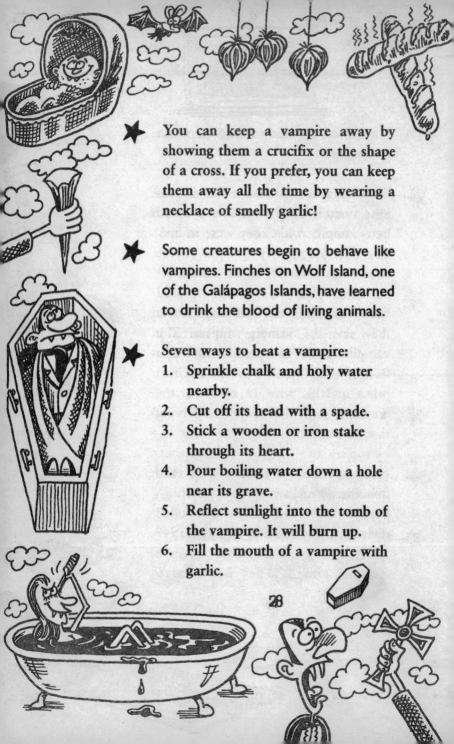

★ You can keep a vampire away by showing them a crucifix or the shape of a cross. If you prefer, you can keep them away all the time by wearing a necklace of smelly garlic!

★ Some creatures begin to behave like vampires. Finches on Wolf Island, one of the Galápagos Islands, have learned to drink the blood of living animals.

★ Seven ways to beat a vampire:
1. Sprinkle chalk and holy water nearby.
2. Cut off its head with a spade.
3. Stick a wooden or iron stake through its heart.
4. Pour boiling water down a hole near its grave.
5. Reflect sunlight into the tomb of the vampire. It will burn up.
6. Fill the mouth of a vampire with garlic.

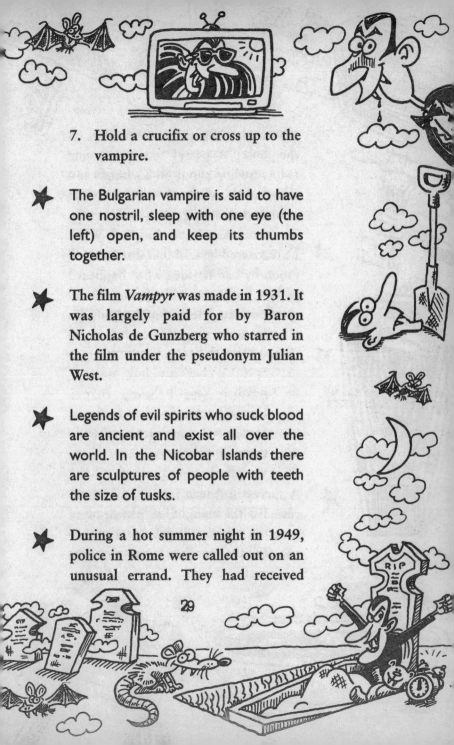

7. Hold a crucifix or cross up to the vampire.

★ The Bulgarian vampire is said to have one nostril, sleep with one eye (the left) open, and keep its thumbs together.

★ The film *Vampyr* was made in 1931. It was largely paid for by Baron Nicholas de Gunzberg who starred in the film under the pseudonym Julian West.

★ Legends of evil spirits who suck blood are ancient and exist all over the world. In the Nicobar Islands there are sculptures of people with teeth the size of tusks.

★ During a hot summer night in 1949, police in Rome were called out on an unusual errand. They had received

29

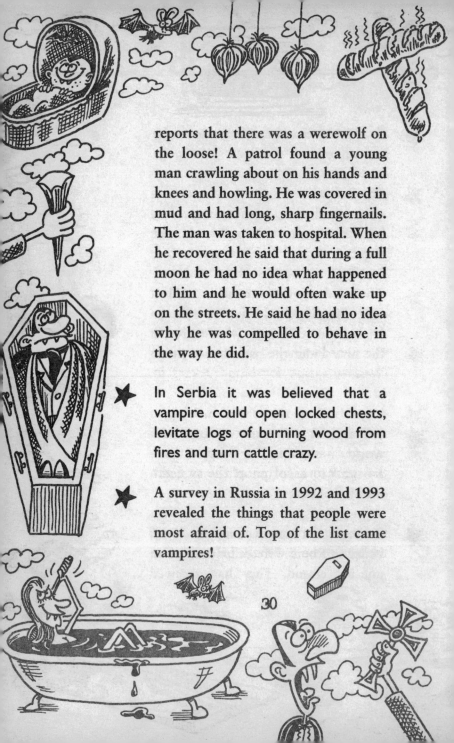

reports that there was a werewolf on the loose! A patrol found a young man crawling about on his hands and knees and howling. He was covered in mud and had long, sharp fingernails. The man was taken to hospital. When he recovered he said that during a full moon he had no idea what happened to him and he would often wake up on the streets. He said he had no idea why he was compelled to behave in the way he did.

★ In Serbia it was believed that a vampire could open locked chests, levitate logs of burning wood from fires and turn cattle crazy.

★ A survey in Russia in 1992 and 1993 revealed the things that people were most afraid of. Top of the list came vampires!

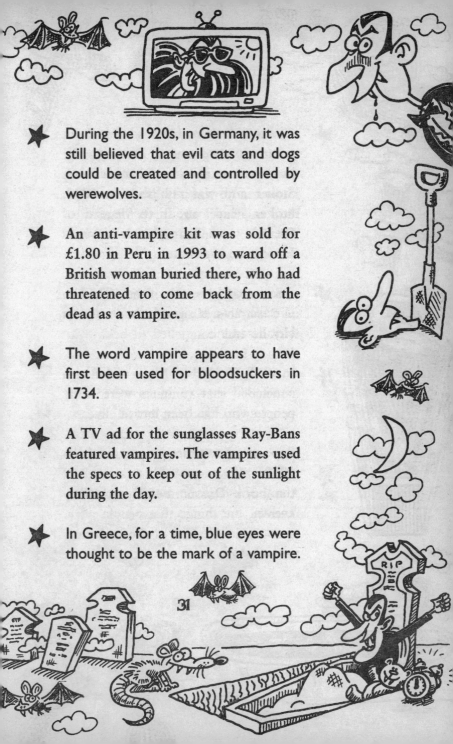

★ During the 1920s, in Germany, it was still believed that evil cats and dogs could be created and controlled by werewolves.

★ An anti-vampire kit was sold for £1.80 in Peru in 1993 to ward off a British woman buried there, who had threatened to come back from the dead as a vampire.

★ The word vampire appears to have first been used for bloodsuckers in 1734.

★ A TV ad for the sunglasses Ray-Bans featured vampires. The vampires used the specs to keep out of the sunlight during the day.

★ In Greece, for a time, blue eyes were thought to be the mark of a vampire.

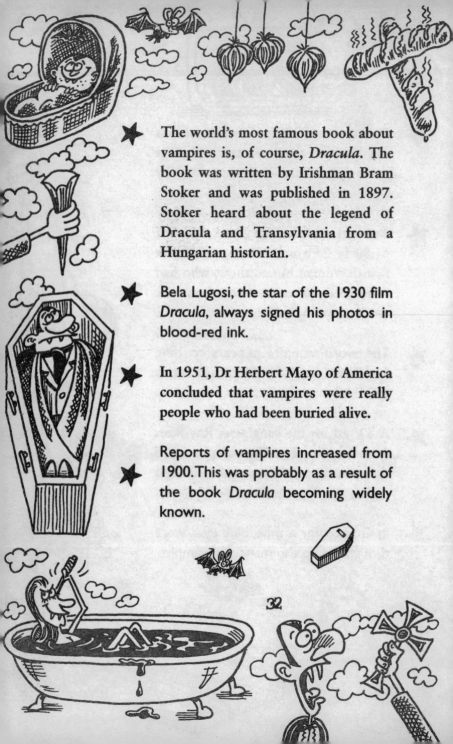

★ The world's most famous book about vampires is, of course, *Dracula*. The book was written by Irishman Bram Stoker and was published in 1897. Stoker heard about the legend of Dracula and Transylvania from a Hungarian historian.

★ Bela Lugosi, the star of the 1930 film *Dracula*, always signed his photos in blood-red ink.

★ In 1951, Dr Herbert Mayo of America concluded that vampires were really people who had been buried alive.

★ Reports of vampires increased from 1900. This was probably as a result of the book *Dracula* becoming widely known.

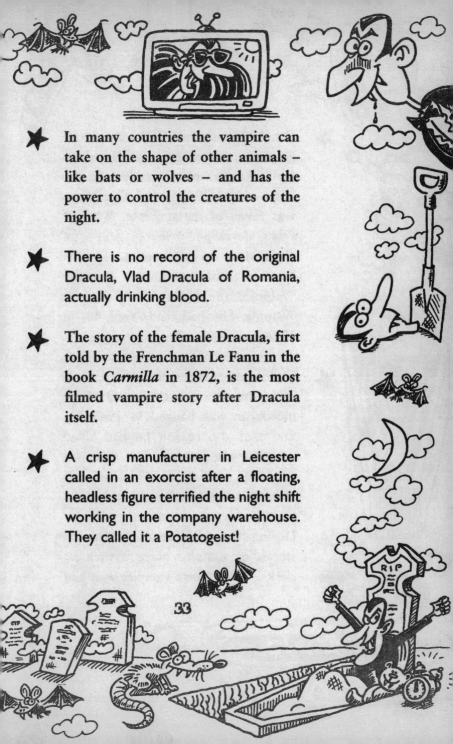

★ In many countries the vampire can take on the shape of other animals – like bats or wolves – and has the power to control the creatures of the night.

★ There is no record of the original Dracula, Vlad Dracula of Romania, actually drinking blood.

★ The story of the female Dracula, first told by the Frenchman Le Fanu in the book *Carmilla* in 1872, is the most filmed vampire story after Dracula itself.

★ A crisp manufacturer in Leicester called in an exorcist after a floating, headless figure terrified the night shift working in the company warehouse. They called it a Potatogeist!

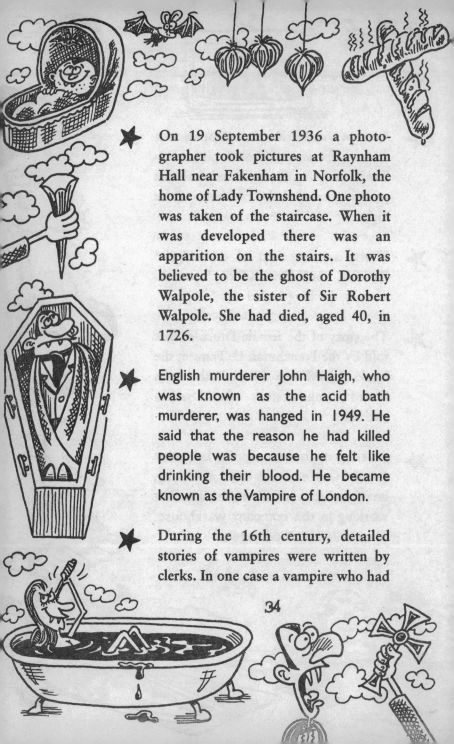

On 19 September 1936 a photographer took pictures at Raynham Hall near Fakenham in Norfolk, the home of Lady Townshend. One photo was taken of the staircase. When it was developed there was an apparition on the stairs. It was believed to be the ghost of Dorothy Walpole, the sister of Sir Robert Walpole. She had died, aged 40, in 1726.

English murderer John Haigh, who was known as the acid bath murderer, was hanged in 1949. He said that the reason he had killed people was because he felt like drinking their blood. He became known as the Vampire of London.

During the 16th century, detailed stories of vampires were written by clerks. In one case a vampire who had

34

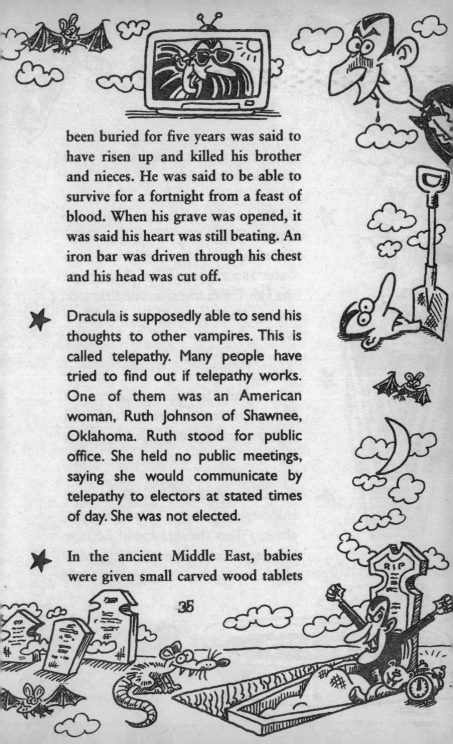

been buried for five years was said to have risen up and killed his brother and nieces. He was said to be able to survive for a fortnight from a feast of blood. When his grave was opened, it was said his heart was still beating. An iron bar was driven through his chest and his head was cut off.

★ Dracula is supposedly able to send his thoughts to other vampires. This is called telepathy. Many people have tried to find out if telepathy works. One of them was an American woman, Ruth Johnson of Shawnee, Oklahoma. Ruth stood for public office. She held no public meetings, saying she would communicate by telepathy to electors at stated times of day. She was not elected.

★ In the ancient Middle East, babies were given small carved wood tablets

35

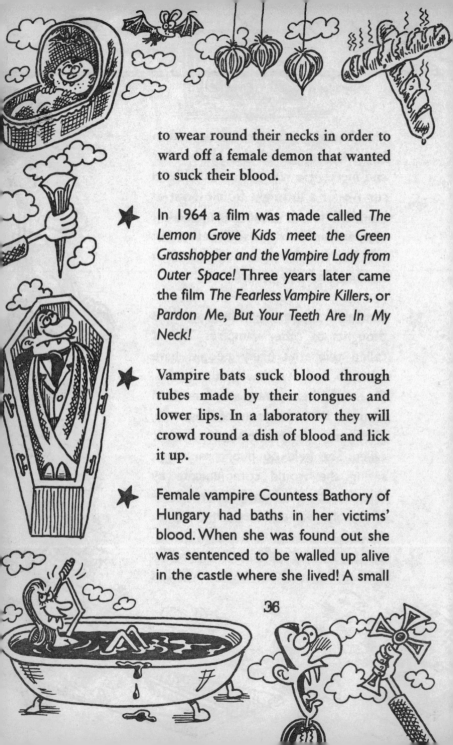

to wear round their necks in order to ward off a female demon that wanted to suck their blood.

★ In 1964 a film was made called *The Lemon Grove Kids meet the Green Grasshopper and the Vampire Lady from Outer Space!* Three years later came the film *The Fearless Vampire Killers*, or *Pardon Me, But Your Teeth Are In My Neck!*

★ Vampire bats suck blood through tubes made by their tongues and lower lips. In a laboratory they will crowd round a dish of blood and lick it up.

★ Female vampire Countess Bathory of Hungary had baths in her victims' blood. When she was found out she was sentenced to be walled up alive in the castle where she lived! A small

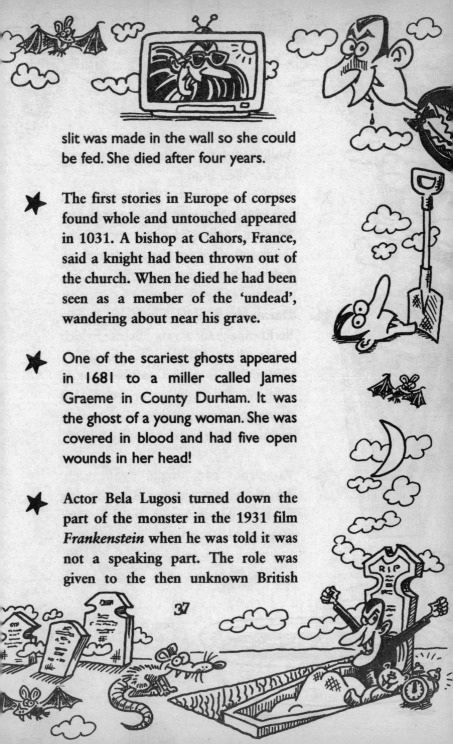

slit was made in the wall so she could be fed. She died after four years.

★ The first stories in Europe of corpses found whole and untouched appeared in 1031. A bishop at Cahors, France, said a knight had been thrown out of the church. When he died he had been seen as a member of the 'undead', wandering about near his grave.

★ One of the scariest ghosts appeared in 1681 to a miller called James Graeme in County Durham. It was the ghost of a young woman. She was covered in blood and had five open wounds in her head!

★ Actor Bela Lugosi turned down the part of the monster in the 1931 film *Frankenstein* when he was told it was not a speaking part. The role was given to the then unknown British

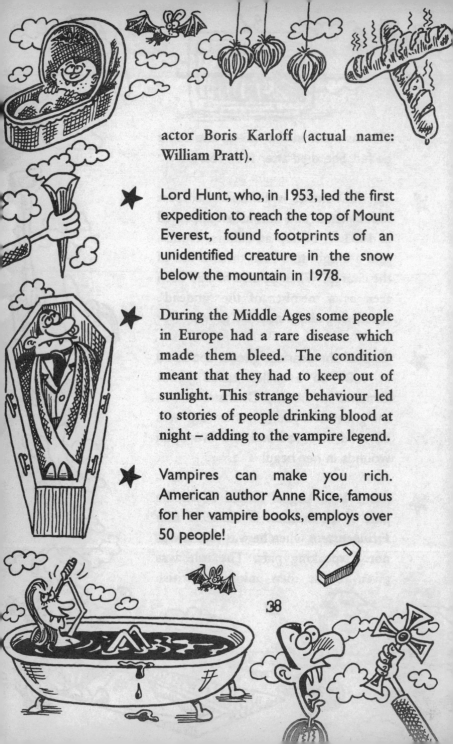

actor Boris Karloff (actual name: William Pratt).

★ Lord Hunt, who, in 1953, led the first expedition to reach the top of Mount Everest, found footprints of an unidentified creature in the snow below the mountain in 1978.

★ During the Middle Ages some people in Europe had a rare disease which made them bleed. The condition meant that they had to keep out of sunlight. This strange behaviour led to stories of people drinking blood at night – adding to the vampire legend.

★ Vampires can make you rich. American author Anne Rice, famous for her vampire books, employs over 50 people!

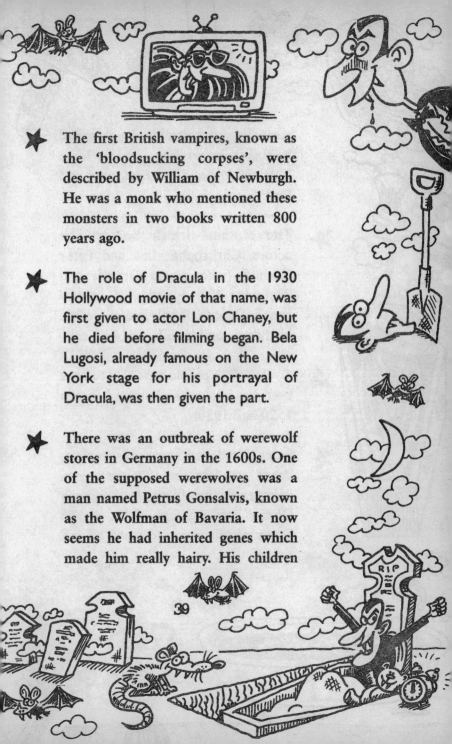

★ The first British vampires, known as the 'bloodsucking corpses', were described by William of Newburgh. He was a monk who mentioned these monsters in two books written 800 years ago.

★ The role of Dracula in the 1930 Hollywood movie of that name, was first given to actor Lon Chaney, but he died before filming began. Bela Lugosi, already famous on the New York stage for his portrayal of Dracula, was then given the part.

★ There was an outbreak of werewolf stores in Germany in the 1600s. One of the supposed werewolves was a man named Petrus Gonsalvis, known as the Wolfman of Bavaria. It now seems he had inherited genes which made him really hairy. His children

were also very hairy. His daughter had hair all over her face – except for a little space round her eyes, nose and lips!

★ The famous British horror film actors, Christopher Lee and Peter Cushing (who played Dracula and Professor Von Helsing in several classic Dracula films), had the same birthday – on May 27.

★ Over 30,000 people were said to have been werewolves in Europe between 1520 and 1650!

★ Fears of evil spirits, not just vampires, lasted well into the 19th century in Britain. Prime Minister Benjamin Disraeli left the legs of his bed in bowls of salt water to ward off evil spirits.

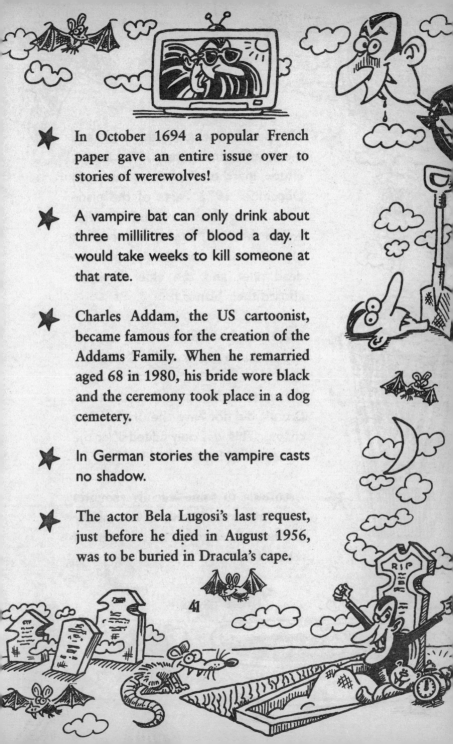

★ In October 1694 a popular French paper gave an entire issue over to stories of werewolves!

★ A vampire bat can only drink about three millilitres of blood a day. It would take weeks to kill someone at that rate.

★ Charles Addam, the US cartoonist, became famous for the creation of the Addams Family. When he remarried aged 68 in 1980, his bride wore black and the ceremony took place in a dog cemetery.

★ In German stories the vampire casts no shadow.

★ The actor Bela Lugosi's last request, just before he died in August 1956, was to be buried in Dracula's cape.

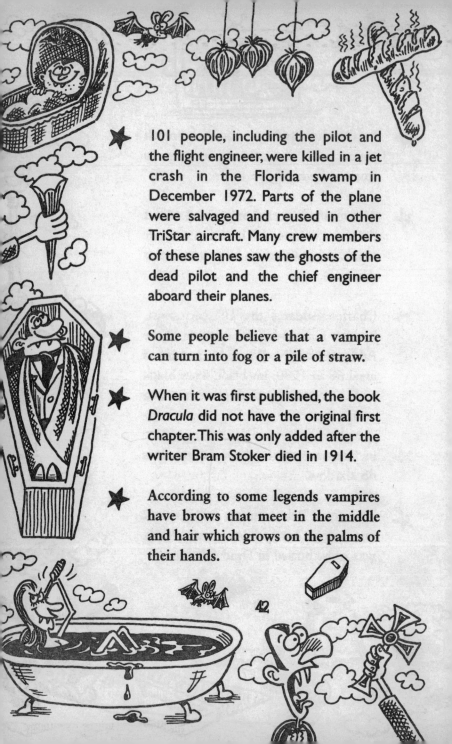

★ 101 people, including the pilot and the flight engineer, were killed in a jet crash in the Florida swamp in December 1972. Parts of the plane were salvaged and reused in other TriStar aircraft. Many crew members of these planes saw the ghosts of the dead pilot and the chief engineer aboard their planes.

★ Some people believe that a vampire can turn into fog or a pile of straw.

★ When it was first published, the book *Dracula* did not have the original first chapter. This was only added after the writer Bram Stoker died in 1914.

★ According to some legends vampires have brows that meet in the middle and hair which grows on the palms of their hands.

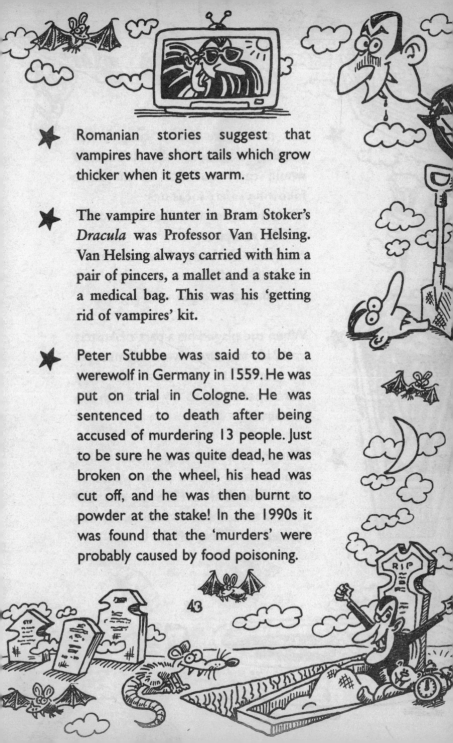

★ Romanian stories suggest that vampires have short tails which grow thicker when it gets warm.

★ The vampire hunter in Bram Stoker's *Dracula* was Professor Van Helsing. Van Helsing always carried with him a pair of pincers, a mallet and a stake in a medical bag. This was his 'getting rid of vampires' kit.

★ Peter Stubbe was said to be a werewolf in Germany in 1559. He was put on trial in Cologne. He was sentenced to death after being accused of murdering 13 people. Just to be sure he was quite dead, he was broken on the wheel, his head was cut off, and he was then burnt to powder at the stake! In the 1990s it was found that the 'murders' were probably caused by food poisoning.

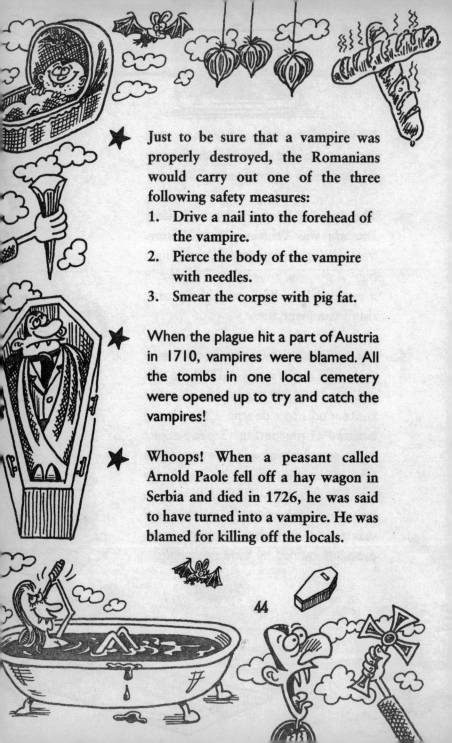

Just to be sure that a vampire was properly destroyed, the Romanians would carry out one of the three following safety measures:

1. Drive a nail into the forehead of the vampire.
2. Pierce the body of the vampire with needles.
3. Smear the corpse with pig fat.

When the plague hit a part of Austria in 1710, vampires were blamed. All the tombs in one local cemetery were opened up to try and catch the vampires!

Whoops! When a peasant called Arnold Paole fell off a hay wagon in Serbia and died in 1726, he was said to have turned into a vampire. He was blamed for killing off the locals.

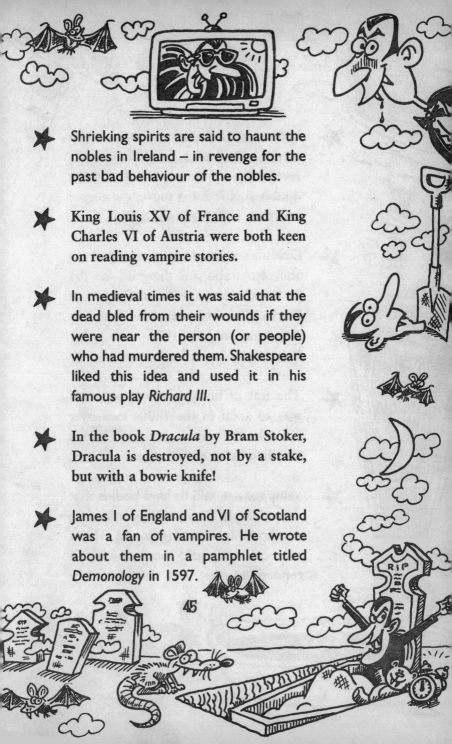

★ Shrieking spirits are said to haunt the nobles in Ireland – in revenge for the past bad behaviour of the nobles.

★ King Louis XV of France and King Charles VI of Austria were both keen on reading vampire stories.

★ In medieval times it was said that the dead bled from their wounds if they were near the person (or people) who had murdered them. Shakespeare liked this idea and used it in his famous play *Richard III*.

★ In the book *Dracula* by Bram Stoker, Dracula is destroyed, not by a stake, but with a bowie knife!

★ James I of England and VI of Scotland was a fan of vampires. He wrote about them in a pamphlet titled *Demonology* in 1597.

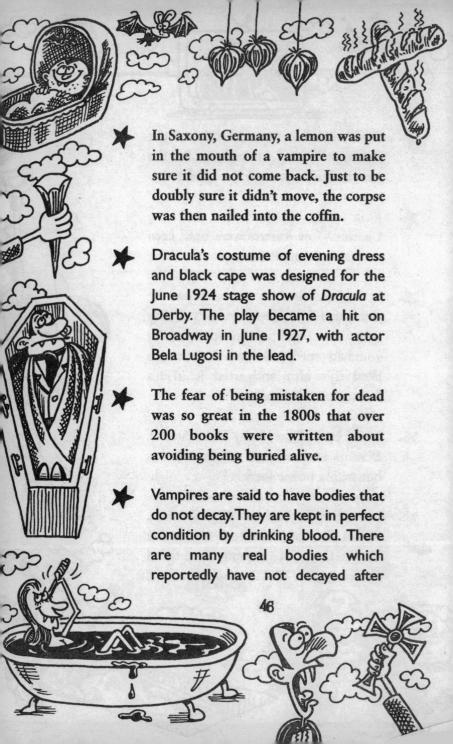

In Saxony, Germany, a lemon was put in the mouth of a vampire to make sure it did not come back. Just to be doubly sure it didn't move, the corpse was then nailed into the coffin.

Dracula's costume of evening dress and black cape was designed for the June 1924 stage show of *Dracula* at Derby. The play became a hit on Broadway in June 1927, with actor Bela Lugosi in the lead.

The fear of being mistaken for dead was so great in the 1800s that over 200 books were written about avoiding being buried alive.

Vampires are said to have bodies that do not decay. They are kept in perfect condition by drinking blood. There are many real bodies which reportedly have not decayed after

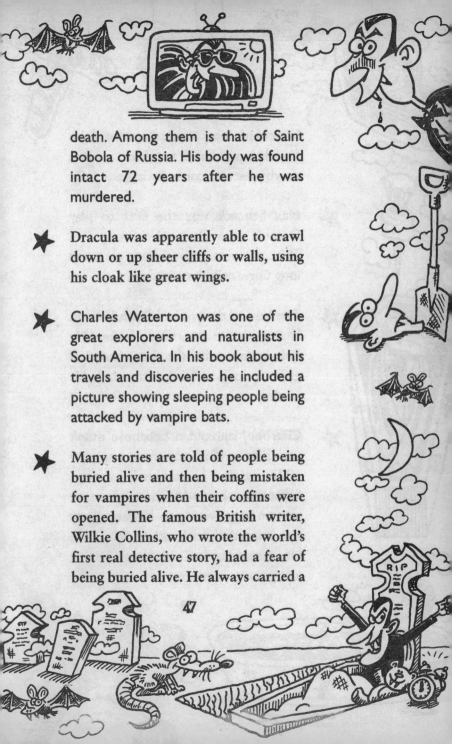

death. Among them is that of Saint Bobola of Russia. His body was found intact 72 years after he was murdered.

★ Dracula was apparently able to crawl down or up sheer cliffs or walls, using his cloak like great wings.

★ Charles Waterton was one of the great explorers and naturalists in South America. In his book about his travels and discoveries he included a picture showing sleeping people being attacked by vampire bats.

★ Many stories are told of people being buried alive and then being mistaken for vampires when their coffins were opened. The famous British writer, Wilkie Collins, who wrote the world's first real detective story, had a fear of being buried alive. He always carried a

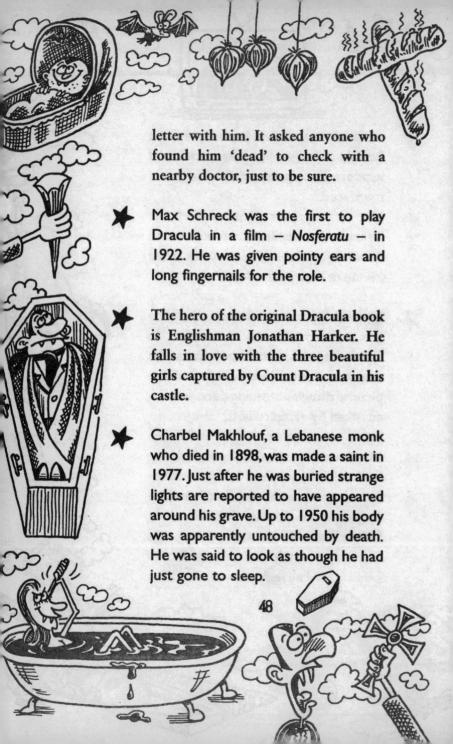

letter with him. It asked anyone who found him 'dead' to check with a nearby doctor, just to be sure.

★ Max Schreck was the first to play Dracula in a film – *Nosferatu* – in 1922. He was given pointy ears and long fingernails for the role.

★ The hero of the original Dracula book is Englishman Jonathan Harker. He falls in love with the three beautiful girls captured by Count Dracula in his castle.

★ Charbel Makhlouf, a Lebanese monk who died in 1898, was made a saint in 1977. Just after he was buried strange lights are reported to have appeared around his grave. Up to 1950 his body was apparently untouched by death. He was said to look as though he had just gone to sleep.

48

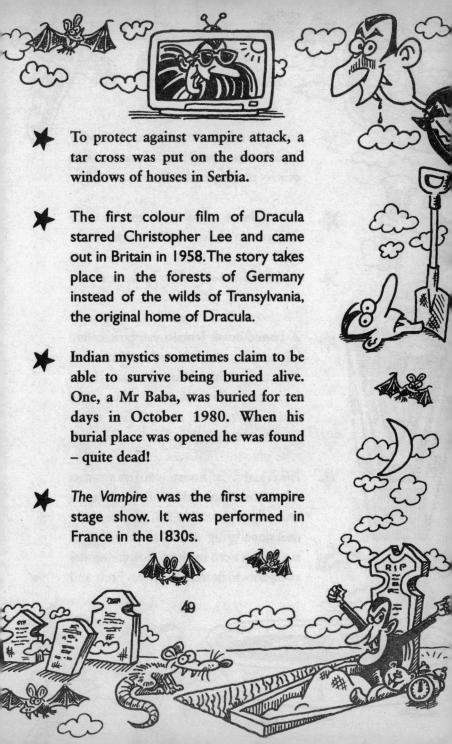

★ To protect against vampire attack, a tar cross was put on the doors and windows of houses in Serbia.

★ The first colour film of Dracula starred Christopher Lee and came out in Britain in 1958. The story takes place in the forests of Germany instead of the wilds of Transylvania, the original home of Dracula.

★ Indian mystics sometimes claim to be able to survive being buried alive. One, a Mr Baba, was buried for ten days in October 1980. When his burial place was opened he was found – quite dead!

★ *The Vampire* was the first vampire stage show. It was performed in France in the 1830s.

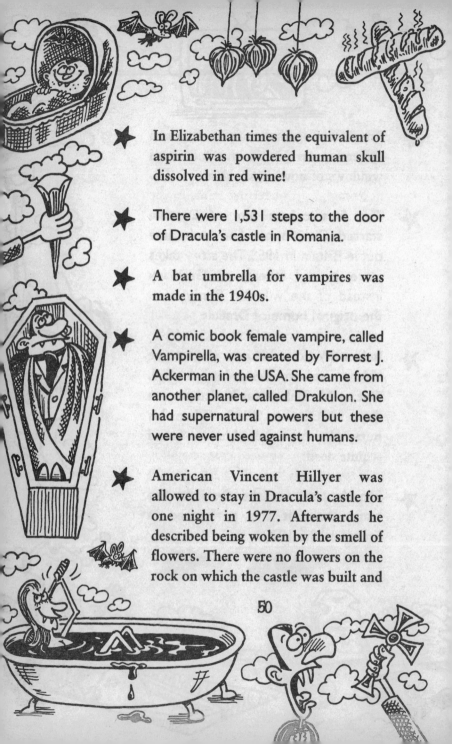

★ In Elizabethan times the equivalent of aspirin was powdered human skull dissolved in red wine!

★ There were 1,531 steps to the door of Dracula's castle in Romania.

★ A bat umbrella for vampires was made in the 1940s.

★ A comic book female vampire, called Vampirella, was created by Forrest J. Ackerman in the USA. She came from another planet, called Drakulon. She had supernatural powers but these were never used against humans.

★ American Vincent Hillyer was allowed to stay in Dracula's castle for one night in 1977. Afterwards he described being woken by the smell of flowers. There were no flowers on the rock on which the castle was built and

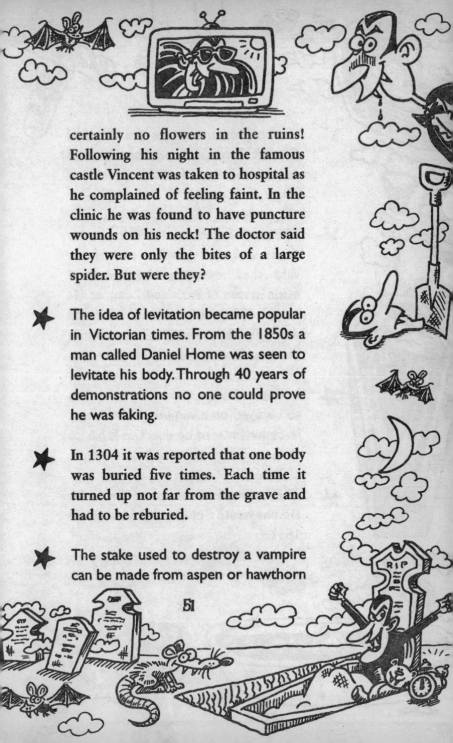

certainly no flowers in the ruins! Following his night in the famous castle Vincent was taken to hospital as he complained of feeling faint. In the clinic he was found to have puncture wounds on his neck! The doctor said they were only the bites of a large spider. But were they?

★ The idea of levitation became popular in Victorian times. From the 1850s a man called Daniel Home was seen to levitate his body. Through 40 years of demonstrations no one could prove he was faking.

★ In 1304 it was reported that one body was buried five times. Each time it turned up not far from the grave and had to be reburied.

★ The stake used to destroy a vampire can be made from aspen or hawthorn

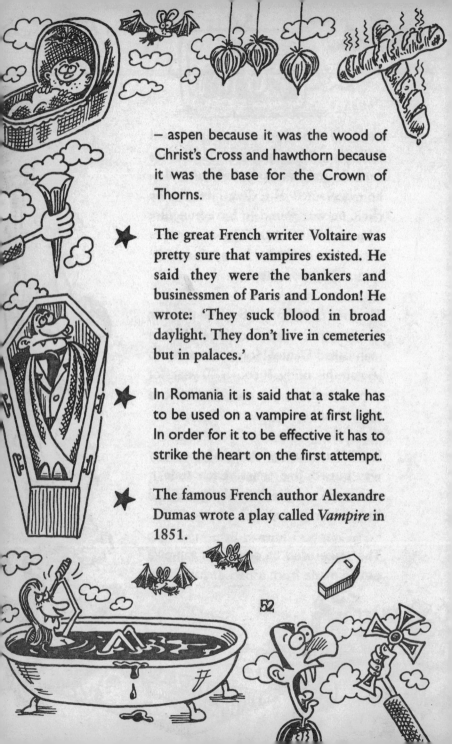

– aspen because it was the wood of Christ's Cross and hawthorn because it was the base for the Crown of Thorns.

The great French writer Voltaire was pretty sure that vampires existed. He said they were the bankers and businessmen of Paris and London! He wrote: 'They suck blood in broad daylight. They don't live in cemeteries but in palaces.'

In Romania it is said that a stake has to be used on a vampire at first light. In order for it to be effective it has to strike the heart on the first attempt.

The famous French author Alexandre Dumas wrote a play called *Vampire* in 1851.

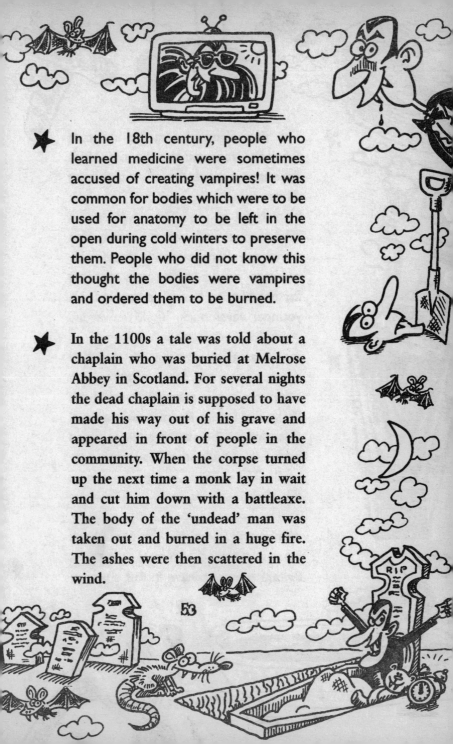

★ In the 18th century, people who learned medicine were sometimes accused of creating vampires! It was common for bodies which were to be used for anatomy to be left in the open during cold winters to preserve them. People who did not know this thought the bodies were vampires and ordered them to be burned.

★ In the 1100s a tale was told about a chaplain who was buried at Melrose Abbey in Scotland. For several nights the dead chaplain is supposed to have made his way out of his grave and appeared in front of people in the community. When the corpse turned up the next time a monk lay in wait and cut him down with a battleaxe. The body of the 'undead' man was taken out and burned in a huge fire. The ashes were then scattered in the wind.

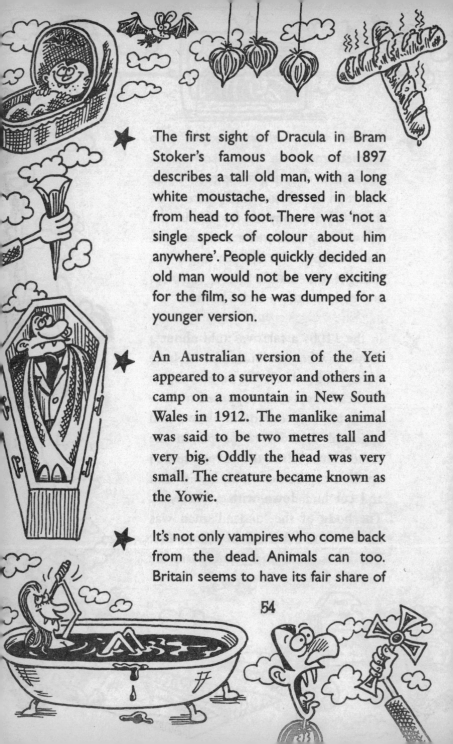

The first sight of Dracula in Bram Stoker's famous book of 1897 describes a tall old man, with a long white moustache, dressed in black from head to foot. There was 'not a single speck of colour about him anywhere'. People quickly decided an old man would not be very exciting for the film, so he was dumped for a younger version.

An Australian version of the Yeti appeared to a surveyor and others in a camp on a mountain in New South Wales in 1912. The manlike animal was said to be two metres tall and very big. Oddly the head was very small. The creature became known as the Yowie.

It's not only vampires who come back from the dead. Animals can too. Britain seems to have its fair share of

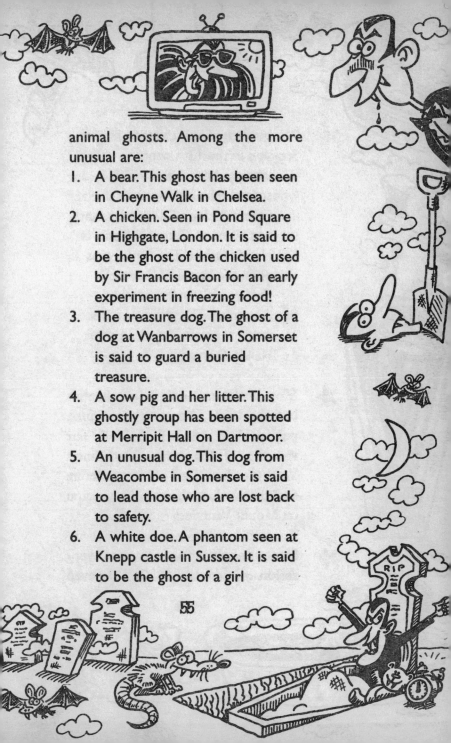

animal ghosts. Among the more unusual are:

1. A bear. This ghost has been seen in Cheyne Walk in Chelsea.

2. A chicken. Seen in Pond Square in Highgate, London. It is said to be the ghost of the chicken used by Sir Francis Bacon for an early experiment in freezing food!

3. The treasure dog. The ghost of a dog at Wanbarrows in Somerset is said to guard a buried treasure.

4. A sow pig and her litter. This ghostly group has been spotted at Merripit Hall on Dartmoor.

5. An unusual dog. This dog from Weacombe in Somerset is said to lead those who are lost back to safety.

6. A white doe. A phantom seen at Knepp castle in Sussex. It is said to be the ghost of a girl

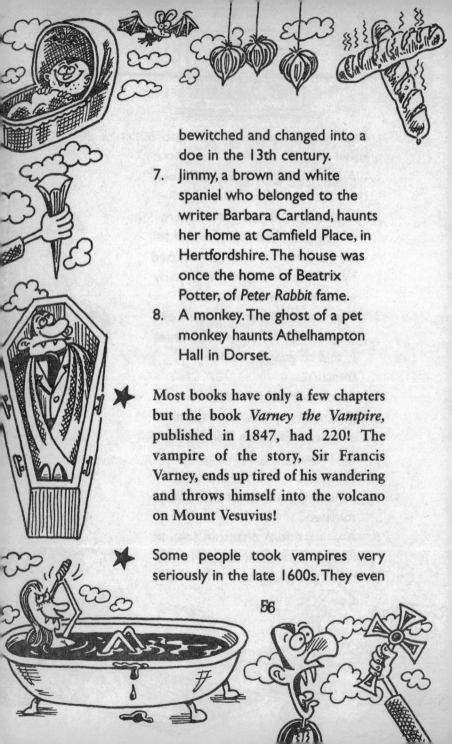

bewitched and changed into a doe in the 13th century.

7. Jimmy, a brown and white spaniel who belonged to the writer Barbara Cartland, haunts her home at Camfield Place, in Hertfordshire. The house was once the home of Beatrix Potter, of *Peter Rabbit* fame.

8. A monkey. The ghost of a pet monkey haunts Athelhampton Hall in Dorset.

Most books have only a few chapters but the book *Varney the Vampire*, published in 1847, had 220! The vampire of the story, Sir Francis Varney, ends up tired of his wandering and throws himself into the volcano on Mount Vesuvius!

Some people took vampires very seriously in the late 1600s. They even

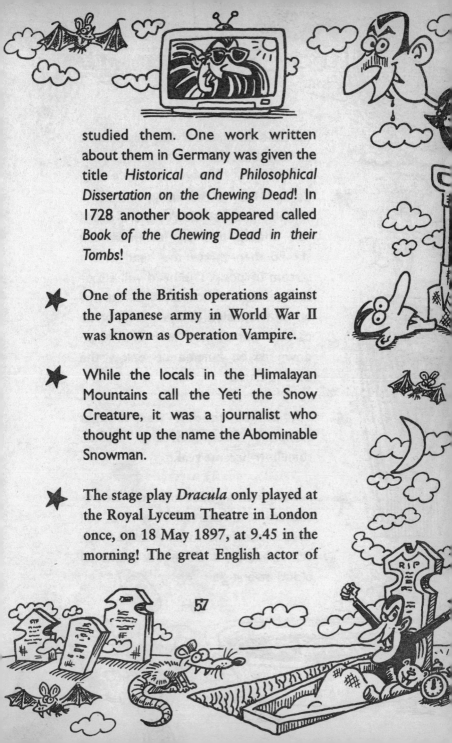

studied them. One work written about them in Germany was given the title *Historical and Philosophical Dissertation on the Chewing Dead!* In 1728 another book appeared called *Book of the Chewing Dead in their Tombs!*

★ One of the British operations against the Japanese army in World War II was known as Operation Vampire.

★ While the locals in the Himalayan Mountains call the Yeti the Snow Creature, it was a journalist who thought up the name the Abominable Snowman.

★ The stage play *Dracula* only played at the Royal Lyceum Theatre in London once, on 18 May 1897, at 9.45 in the morning! The great English actor of

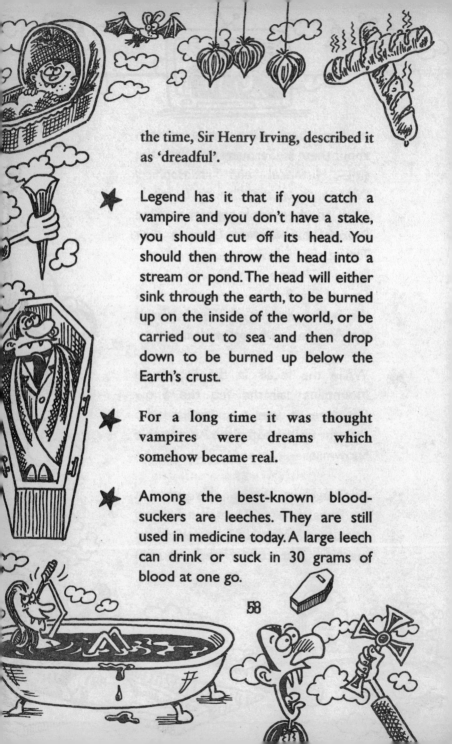

the time, Sir Henry Irving, described it as 'dreadful'.

★ Legend has it that if you catch a vampire and you don't have a stake, you should cut off its head. You should then throw the head into a stream or pond. The head will either sink through the earth, to be burned up on the inside of the world, or be carried out to sea and then drop down to be burned up below the Earth's crust.

★ For a long time it was thought vampires were dreams which somehow became real.

★ Among the best-known blood-suckers are leeches. They are still used in medicine today. A large leech can drink or suck in 30 grams of blood at one go.

58

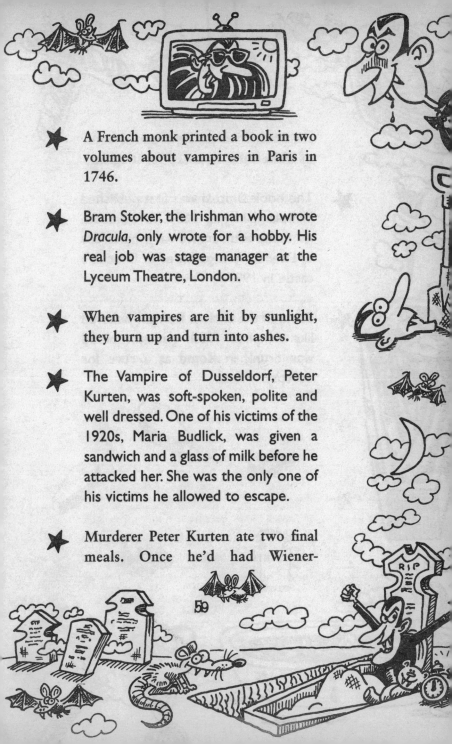

* A French monk printed a book in two volumes about vampires in Paris in 1746.

* Bram Stoker, the Irishman who wrote *Dracula*, only wrote for a hobby. His real job was stage manager at the Lyceum Theatre, London.

* When vampires are hit by sunlight, they burn up and turn into ashes.

* The Vampire of Dusseldorf, Peter Kurten, was soft-spoken, polite and well dressed. One of his victims of the 1920s, Maria Budlick, was given a sandwich and a glass of milk before he attacked her. She was the only one of his victims he allowed to escape.

* Murderer Peter Kurten ate two final meals. Once he'd had Wiener-

schnitzel, fried potatoes and a bottle of white wine, he asked for it again!

★ The book *Dracula* was first published in Ireland in May 1897. To celebrate its hundredth anniversary, hundreds of Dracula fans gathered at Dracula's castle in 1997.

★ Some of the ancient Romans behaved like vampires. Fresh gladiator blood was drunk in Rome as a cure for epilepsy.

Also published by Macmillan

FACT ATTACK

Awesome Aliens

Did you know that . . .

Up to 30,000 tonnes of cosmic dust fall on the
Earth each year.

A study by a doctor in the 1980s found that
small specks of dirt or dust in the eyes can
sometimes be mistaken for UFOs.

In Arès, France, a safe landing spot for UFOs
has been built. It is called the Ovniport.

A Florida insurance company offers insurance
against alien abduction.

The smells said to be inside an alien UFO
include sulphur, pepper and petrol.

Also published by Macmillan

FACT ATTACK

FANTASTIC FOOTBALL

DID YOU KNOW THAT . . .

James I of England was probably the first king to
attend a game of football.

In the 1966 World Cup final, Geoff Hurst scored
three goals – one with a header, one with his left
foot and one with his right foot!

FACT ATTACK

BEASTLY BODIES

DID YOU KNOW THAT . . .

The human body loses enough heat in an hour to boil half a gallon of water.

If calcium is taken out of human bones, they become so rubbery that they can be tied in a knot like rope or string.

The city with the highest number of babies born in taxis is New York, USA.

A giraffe has the same number of bones in its neck as a human does.

Richard III of England, Louis XIV of France and the Emperor Napoleon of France were all born with teeth.

Fact Attack titles available from Macmillan

The prices shown below are correct at the time of going to press.
However, Macmillan Publishers reserve the right to show new retail prices
on covers which may differ from those previously advertised.

Awesome Aliens	0 330 35340 3	£1.99
Beastly Bodies	0 330 35341 1	£1.99
Cool Cars	0 330 35345 4	£1.99
Cracking Christmas	0 330 37504 0	£1.99
Crazy Creatures	0 330 35342 X	£1.99
Crucial Cricket	0 330 37498 2	£1.99
Dastardly Deeds	0 330 35344 6	£1.99
Deadly Deep	0 330 37500 8	£1.99
Devastating Dinosaurs	0 330 37495 8	£1.99
Dreadful Disasters	0 330 35347 0	£1.99
Fantastic Football	0 330 35343 8	£1.99
Gruesome Ghosts	0 330 35346 2	£1.99
Incredible Inventions	0 330 37494 X	£1.99
Mad Medicine	0 330 37082 0	£1.99
Magnificent Monarchs	0 330 37496 6	£1.99
Nutty Numbers	0 330 35434 5	£1.99
Remarkable Rescues	0 330 37502 4	£1.99
Rowdy Rugby	0 330 37501 6	£1.99
Spectacular Space	0 330 37497 4	£1.99
Super Spies	0 330 37499 0	£1.99
Vile Vampires	0 330 37503 2	£1.99

All Macmillan titles can be ordered at your local bookshop
or are available by post from:

Book Service by Post
PO Box 29, Douglas, Isle of Man IM99 1BQ

Credit cards accepted. For details:
Telephone: 01624 675137
Fax: 01624 670923
E-mail: bookshop@enterprise.net

Free postage and packing in the UK.
Overseas customers: add £1 per book (paperback)
and £3 per book (hardback).